# NOTTINGHAMSHIRE
# MEMORIES

DOUGLAS WHITWORTH

SUTTON PUBLISHING

First published in the United Kingdom in 1999 by
Sutton Publishing Limited · Phoenix Mill
Thrupp · Stroud · Gloucestershire · GL5 2BU

British Library Cataloguing in Publication Data
A catalogue record for this book is available from the British Library.

ISBN 0-7509-2070-X

To May and Dorrie

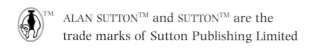 ™ ALAN SUTTON™ and SUTTON™ are the
trade marks of Sutton Publishing Limited

Typeset in 11/14pt Photina.
Typesetting and origination by
Sutton Publishing Limited.
Printed in Great Britain by
WBC Ltd, Bridgend.

# Contents

# Introduction

The photographs in this book are not merely a collection of prints of Nottinghamshire but are, in the main, one man's view of the county. That man was Frank Walden Stevenson, a photographer whose images of the first sixty years of the twentieth century are still fresh and have a powerful impact.

He was a dedicated photographer all his adult life, from 1905 when his father gave him a camera – with the intention of helping to strengthen his eyesight by compelling him to concentrate his vision on a particular object. His great friends Harold Caunton and Leonard Harrison caught his enthusiasm for travelling around the Nottinghamshire and Derbyshire lanes and byways taking photographs, and all three soon became very proficient with their cameras.

Until the 1920s Frank Stevenson remained an amateur photographer, but following his success in winning a photographic competition held by the *Nottingham Journal* in 1927 he was frequently sent on assignments by the newspaper. This led, in 1929, to an offer to join the newspaper as a staff photographer on a permanent basis, and during the 1930s he widened his experience of Nottinghamshire people and events.

On the retirement of Freddie Foxton, a volatile Yorkshireman and a true friend, Frank Stevenson was appointed the senior staff photographer on the *Journal*. The decision of the editor to have an entire page of pictures at the back of the newspaper brought much

Frank Stevenson, on the right, whose photographs form the basis for this book, and Harold Caunton, his friend, on a photographic expedition to Lambley, 1911. Although he occasionally used a roll-film camera, the majority of Frank Stevenson's work was accomplished with a glass-plate camera, which although cumbersome allowed him time to compose his pictures. Harold Caunton was tragically killed in one of the first offensives of the First World War.

A May Day parade on the Forest Recreation Ground, 1950s. The parade, which was organised by local trade unions, travelled from the Old Market Square and ended on the Forest where the judging of the decorated floats took place.

praise and recognition from its readers. They appreciated not only the pictures, some topical, some landscapes and others portraits of well-known Nottinghamshire public figures, but also the captions, which had a style and humour of their own, reflecting Frank's lifetime of reading. In those days photographers' work was not acknowledged in newspapers, but Frank's contributions could be picked out unerringly by those who had seen his entries in local photographic exhibitions.

Frank taught Edgar Lloyd and Norman Boot, who were new photographers on the *Journal*, and was proud of their progress. All three of them, in addition to Bert Weller of the *Nottingham Guardian*, were the best of friends, sharing the ups and downs of a cameraman's daily life – the scoops and the occasional disappointments. Bert Weller and Frank Stevenson became familiar figures in Bert's little Morgan car, which carried them hundreds of miles round Nottinghamshire on their assignments.

As a press photographer, Frank covered a wide variety of events, including meetings, functions and sporting fixtures, but he never lost his love of pictorial photography. As the years passed and changing circumstances began to alter the face of Nottingham, he foresaw that many public buildings and old houses would vanish for ever if they were not captured in photographs. He searched out and recorded all the old parts of the city, and his photographs have become a chronicle of the first half of the twentieth century.

He was more than a press photographer, he was a friend and adviser to many a distinguished public figure. When a Lord Mayor attending a Jewish funeral removed his hat, Frank whispered to him to put it back on his head as it was the Jewish custom!

In 1949, at the age of fifty-eight, Frank embarked on his most ambitious project – to become an Associate of the Royal Photographic Society. It was a marathon effort, taking well over a year to complete, but in 1951 he was awarded his Associateship and two of the twelve entries he submitted were chosen by the RPS to be hung in their gallery at the summer exhibition.

Frank was a much respected figure when in 1955 he decided to retire from the *Nottingham Journal*, but he continued to record the local scene until his death in 1964.

His work, although having the appearance of spontaneity, was always studied: he had endless patience and would wait for exactly the right moment to take his photographs.

Frank Stevenson rarely photographed the coal mines and miners of Nottinghamshire, but he covered most other aspects of the life and landscape of the county, travelling the length and breadth of the shire.

Nottingham is not well situated for a county town, but was the natural site for a settlement in the Middle Ages, having a ford over the River Trent and a rock escarpment on the summit of which the earliest inhabitants made their home. The Saxons were the first to build here, in the area where St Mary's Church now stands, followed by the Danes who brought their own system of law. When the Normans came in the eleventh century they constructed a fort of timber and earth on the hill to the west – the two districts acquiring the titles of the English and the French Boroughs respectively. Gradually the two settlements merged, but the Borough of Nottingham never extended beyond the medieval town wall for the next 800 years.

Modern Nottingham is the product of four phases. After the enclosure of the Burgesses' land beyond the town wall in 1845, building of terraced houses went ahead in the inner suburbs of the Meadows and St Ann's. In 1877 Nottingham acquired the suburbs of Basford, Bulwell, Lenton, Radford, Carrington and Sneinton, thereby doubling the population of the borough.

Nottingham achieved the status of a city in 1897, but it was not until after the First World War that the city authorities began the demolition of the packed houses in Broad Marsh, Narrow Marsh and Sneinton Bottoms which had so discredited Nottingham's reputation. New estates of council houses were then built in the north and west of the city: Stockhill Lane Estate was the first, followed by Sherwood, Aspley and Broxtowe, the latter being finished after the Second World War. Even as late as the 1930s Aspley Lane was a pleasant country road, bordered by a fine avenue of trees along which residents enjoyed strolling or cycling.

The last major development in the city took place in the 1950s–70s. During that period the Clifton housing estate was built and much of St Ann's and the Meadows was redeveloped. Most controversially, the two city centre shopping centres and Maid Marian Way were constructed, thereby causing the demolition of several historic properties. Although almost a thousand years old, Nottingham has very few buildings remaining from the Middle Ages, the urge to modernise having been put before historical considerations.

This last century has also seen great changes in transport. The first decade of the twentieth century saw the last horse buses on Nottingham's roads. Electric tramcars were introduced in 1901 and remained for less than forty years, to be followed by trolley-buses which served for approximately the same length of time. Both these forms of transport had their enthusiasts. A modern tramway system is planned for Nottingham in the twenty-first century – the city's hills being no problem for modern trams.

The county has little in the way of dramatic scenery – Creswell Crags, which it shares with Derbyshire in the north-west, is perhaps the exception. Nottinghamshire does have, however, a variety of landscapes created by the geological structure within its borders. Towards the north of the county lies Sherwood Forest, and although it no longer has the extensive woodlands of the Middle Ages, when it covered an area of 200 square miles, remains of it still exist in the Dukeries. This area of Nottinghamshire, which was famous for its great Ducal estates, has now become largely an area for leisure pursuits. Although not ducal seats, Rufford Abbey and Newstead Abbey have been opened to the public by the local authorities and Clumber Park is now a National Trust property.

To the west of the forest and straddling the border with Derbyshire is the hilly countryside which was strewn with collieries and miners' houses until the sudden rush of pit closures in the 1980s. The waste heaps and the few remaining collieries are the only evidence of the great industry of this part of Nottinghamshire. Away from the M1 motorway some parts of this area are still visually the same as described by D.H. Lawrence in his novels, but by 1926, on his last visit to Eastwood, he saw the changes which were already occurring in this region.

Mansfield is the largest town in the area, and from being greatly dependent on the coal industry for its prosperity, its fortune is now linked to a variety of trades. The completion of the Robin Hood Line provides a rail link between Nottingham and Worksop, and has brought the villages and towns of the former coalfield area on to the rail network.

East of Sherwood Forest, towards Southwell, is perhaps the most attractive landscape in the county. This is the area traversed by valleys down which streams known as dumbles or becks run. Outings to this part of the shire were regular treats in the past, perhaps ending with tea taken in Lambley or Woodborough.

Southwell, on the edge of this distinctive landscape, is regarded by many as the most beautiful town in the county. Besides having the great Norman Minster, which still comes as a surprise in such a small town, there are many fine Georgian houses in the nearby streets.

The market town of Newark-on-Trent, which lies on the edge of the Lincolnshire plain, is another town of supreme architectural and historical interest. During the Civil War, Newark – as the local headquarters of the Royalists – endured three sieges by the Parliamentarians, and at the end of the war the great castle was slighted, leaving only a romantic ruin.

In the north of the county, Worksop and Retford are more prosaic towns. However, Worksop has an outstanding fourteenth-century priory gatehouse and Retford possesses a fine Victorian town hall together with many impressive Georgian houses. Blyth is a charming village and, since the Great North Road which passed through the village has been superseded by the nearby A1, the wide main street has a peaceful air.

To the north-east is a small area of Nottinghamshire which is little known – a spur into Lincolnshire on the right bank of the River Trent. The land is flat and featureless, but the villages of Thorney and North and South Clifton are worth exploring.

The River Trent runs through the county for only a third of its entire length, but the people of Nottinghamshire regard it as their river. Some stretches of the river have a dull aspect, but the reach from Stoke Bardolph to Rolleston is very pretty and has always attracted crowds of people at weekends.

South of the river, in the flat hedge and ditch countryside of the Vale of Belvoir, are many small and pretty villages set 2 or 3 miles apart – all with their distinctive churches. Perhaps the prettiest village of them all is Car Colston, which has two village greens with delightful houses scattered round them. Dr Robert Thoroton, who was the first historian of Nottinghamshire, lived in Morin Hall in the village and is buried in the local churchyard.

Towards the Leicestershire border are the Wolds, which give fine views over the surrounding countryside. Although known as the Leicestershire Wolds, this stretch of land adds to the diversity of landscape which Nottinghamshire possesses. Although Nottingham dominates the county commercially, culturally and administratively, the towns and villages of Nottinghamshire all have their own individuality which their inhabitants are endeavouring to retain. Towards the north of the county particularly, there is a feeling of being remote from the central authority, but a tradition of belonging to a shire created a thousand years ago is a powerful force to change.

Frank Stevenson's photographs portray the many facets of Nottinghamshire life and scenes during the first six decades of a century that has seen more changes than any in the millennium.

# Nottingham

The Goose Fair, 1914. The fair was the great event of the year in the market place and this picture shows some of the attractions that drew the crowds. From this time onwards, the fair was dominated by the big riding machines, and Collins' roundabouts were among the most prominent. Two of the massive and noisy steam engines that were employed to bring the roundabouts and shows to the fair and to generate power for them are in the right foreground. The fair extended into all the surrounding streets, and an overflow fair was often held in Sneinton.

The unveiling of the statue of Queen Victoria by the Duchess of Portland in the Great Market Place, 28 July 1905. Although it was not a public holiday, the streets from the Midland Railway station, where the Duke and Duchess arrived, were crowded with people wishing to see the Duke's procession. Four years after Queen Victoria's death public feeling for her was still great, and statues and memorials in her memory were being erected throughout the country.

The Duke and Duchess of Portland arriving at the Exchange for a reception prior to the unveiling of the statue of Queen Victoria. The Exchange block, which housed the mayor's parlour and offices, also included five public houses, the butchers' stalls known as the Shambles, several shops, the Police Office and the residence of the mayor's sergeant.

The statue of Queen Victoria after the unveiling ceremony. The sculptor was Albert Toft. Before the final site for the statue was approved a mock statue was made, and was positioned in various parts of the square to discover the most suitable place for it. The position finally chosen, at the west end of the market place, was known as the Stones, where the pot market was located. The statue remained there for forty-eight years, when it was removed to the Victoria Embankment Memorial Gardens.

The Trip to Jerusalem in Brewhouse Yard, 1906. The date of 1189 now painted on the outside of the inn possibly refers to the original foundation of an ale house beneath the castle. The name Trip to Jerusalem first appeared in a list of the town's inns published in a directory of 1799; previously the inn was known as the Pilgrim.

The Gate Hangs Well, Brewhouse Yard, in 1906, the year in which it closed. The sign outside reads 'This gate hangs well, and hinders none, refresh and pay, and travel on'. This sixteenth-century inn, owned by the Duke of Newcastle, was also once known as the Hanging Gate, and following the withdrawal of its licence was demolished in 1909.

The Salutation Inn, 1904. This inn, one of the oldest in Nottingham, has now been extended and modernised, but the interior still retains much of its earlier character and underneath there is an extensive cave system. St Nicholas Street on the left was called Jew Lane in the thirteenth century – a name derived from the number of Jews living in a ghetto in this part of the town.

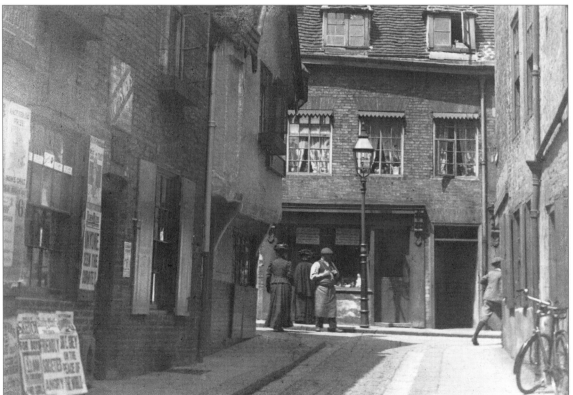

The Salutation Inn, on the left, at the corner of St Nicholas Street and Hounds Gate, 1913. The newsagent's shop in the left foreground has bill-boards advertising now-defunct publications such as *Answers*, *Home Chat*, *John Bull* and the *Daily Sketch*. The poster for the *Nottingham Guardian* is advertising an article by Sir Edward Grey, the Foreign Secretary, on 'The Peace of the World', which was soon to be shattered by the First World War.

The Riding School on Castle Road, 1906. The school was built in 1798 for the Nottingham Troop of the Yeomanry Cavalry and enlarged in 1874 for the Robin Hood Rifles. During the nineteenth century the school was also used by strolling players. The building was later utilised as a sorting office for Christmas mail and as a store for food during the First World War. It was demolished in 1926.

Nottingham Castle and the wharves on the Nottingham Canal, *c.* 1900. When Castle Boulevard was built in 1884 the River Leen, which until then ran close to the castle rock, was diverted and culverted, and the Park Wharf Basin on the nearby canal was also filled in.

Spaniel Row and Friar Lane, c. 1900. The corner house was once owned by Sheriff John Reckless who in 1649 gave shelter here to George Fox, the Quaker, after his imprisonment for disturbing a service in St Mary's Church. The house later became the first Friends Meeting House in Nottingham. All these properties were demolished in the early 1920s when Friar Lane was widened.

Wentworth's funeral hearse outside their premises on Derby Road, c. 1900. Wentworth's undertaking business began in 1832 and was later purchased by C.W. Girvan who also hired out horse brakes and coaches. In 1903 Richard Clower, who began as an undertaker in 1888, acquired the business and he, and later his four sons, ran the company until 1945 when it was sold to the Nottingham Co-operative Society.

A horse-drawn fire engine entering the Guildhall drill yard, c. 1900. All the city's fire appliances were horse-drawn until 1911 when two 75 h.p. Dennis motor fire engines were acquired. In 1919 a motorised turntable ladder appliance costing £3,250 was added to the fleet. The Guildhall was built in 1888 and has remained largely unaltered, but the two ornate lamps in this photograph have been removed.

New Yard, 1905. William Abednego Thompson, known as Bendigo, was born in 1811 in the house with three steps outside. He began prize-fighting for a living at the age of twenty-one, and during his career of eighteen years he lost only one fight. His life became a slow decline into alcoholism, until in 1872, after hearing the evangelist Richard Weaver preaching, he was converted – and the last few years of his life were devoted to evangelism. New Yard was later renamed Trinity Walk and was redeveloped in the 1930s. The spire of Holy Trinity Church, in the background, was removed in 1942 after it was found to be unsafe.

The Nottingham School of Art, *c.* 1900. This school, built in 1863–5 in the Italian style by Frederick Bakewell, taught young people the art of design. On the right a young woman is pushing a Victorian perambulator – perhaps taking her infant to the nearby Arboretum.

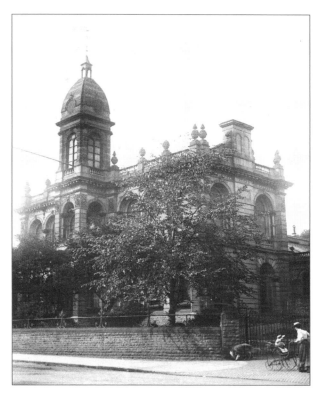

The Midlands Industrial Exhibition from Trent Bridge, 1903. The main building was dedicated almost entirely to exhibits from around the world. There was, however, a multitude of other attractions, including a Canadian Water Chute, an American Roller Coaster, a concert hall, sideshows, an electric theatre, a maze and Blondin II, a high-wire walker. The Roller Coaster was advertised as being a great aid to digestion! The inclusive admission charge to all the attractions was 1*s* 6*d*. The exhibition, which was intended to last for five years, unfortunately remained for only one year – being burnt down in July 1904.

The Great Market Place, *c.* 1905. Electric trams running down the middle of the road are taken in their stride by these pedestrians. This is market day and people have come into the city from all the suburbs and nearby villages. When, in the 1920s, the Corporation planned to remove the market from the city centre, there was an outcry that a centuries-old tradition was to be ended.

Angel Row, 1905. The house in the middle is Bromley House, built by Sir George Smith in 1752 and the family's residence until 1804. For a while it was a draper's shop and then in 1819 the yeomanry used it as a billet during the disturbances of that time. The Nottingham Subscription Library bought the house in 1820 for £2,750, and it became their home the following year.

Wheeler Gate and St Peter's Church, *c.* 1908. Electric trams, which had revolutionised transport in the city, had been on the streets of Nottingham since 1901, but horse buses were still in service on the West Bridgford route: one is in the background at the St Peter's Square terminus. St Peter's Church is one of three Nottingham churches with a history stretching back to Norman times, the others being St Mary's and St Nicholas'. St Peter's was founded by William Peverel to serve the Norman borough, but the present building dates back to around 1250 when the church was completely rebuilt.

Sir John Rees electioneering in Alfred Street South, 1912. In April of that year Captain J.A. Morrison, Conservative and Unionist MP for the Eastern Division of Nottingham, was obliged to resign his seat because of ill health and applied for the Chiltern Hundreds. In the resulting by-election Sir John Rees had a majority of 1,324. Here, Sir John is standing in a horse brake, haranguing a crowd, mostly men, who without exception are all wearing hats. To the left is a men's cast-iron urinal, a piece of Victorian street furniture that has now completely disappeared.

*Opposite*: London Road, *c.* 1900. On the right is Boots Cash Chemists: this shop was opened in 1893, and was the fifth branch to be opened in Nottingham – the beginning of Jesse Boot's expansion both in Nottingham and local towns. The window display is typical of his method at that time – to buy in bulk and sell cheaply. At the bottom of Hollow Stone is the LNWR Goods Depot; the railway station itself was some distance away in Sneinton.

The Postern Gate Inn at the corner of Middle Pavement and Drury Hill, *c.* 1901. The inn, which was built around 1600, was originally named the Bull's Head and later the Golden Fleece. This was the site of the postern that guarded the entrance to the town at this point, and as late as the nineteenth century an iron gate still existed here. The postern was closed at night, the licensee of the inn having charge of the gate bolt. This inn was demolished in 1911 and Postern Chambers, which became a post office, was built on the site.

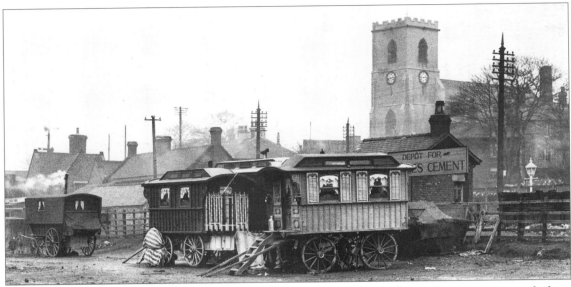

A gipsy camp behind Highbury Road, Bulwell, 1922. These traditional travelling vans are parked on wasteland behind the Midland Railway station. Encampments such as this are now rarely seen in Nottingham: showmen's caravans parked on the Forest for Goose Fair are today mainly in the luxury class.

An elephant from Bostock and Wombwell's Travelling Zoo getting a brush down, 1926. The menagerie had a prime position in the Goose Fair between the statue of Queen Victoria and Market Street. The procession of vans and cages into Nottingham, led by the elephants, was pure showmanship and an attraction in itself. An auction of the animals took place when the menagerie closed in 1931.

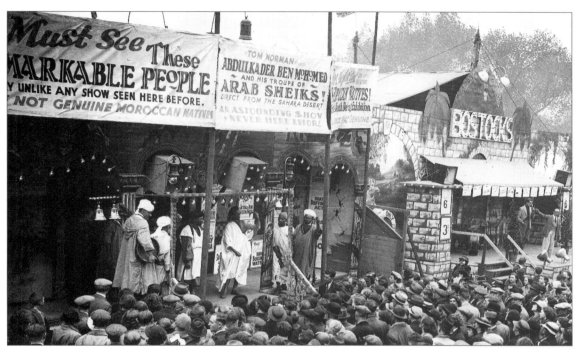

An Arabian show at the Goose Fair on the Forest, 1930. The signs describe the troupe as Arab Sheiks who perform death-defying acts, but no details are given!

Arthur Dexter, the Nottingham Forest goalkeeper, saving a goal in the last minute of the FA Cup fifth round match against Sunderland, 1930. The match, played at Roker Park, Sunderland, in front of a crowd of 45,000, ended in a 2–2 draw. Nottingham Forest won the replay 3–1, but in the sixth round, after a 2–2 draw at home against Sheffield Wednesday, they lost the replay at Hillsborough 3–1.

Sneinton Market, 1931. In the years of the Depression this market, where most articles could be bought at bargain prices, was a great attraction for the needy. After the nearby slum properties were demolished in the 1930s, a new wholesale fruit and vegetable market was built. In 1995 this market was relocated in Meadow Lane, and the area has now been redeveloped with the accent on retail outlets, although the open-air market has been retained.

A charabanc party outside the Elite Picture Theatre, 1924. This cinema, which opened in 1921, was hailed as the finest example of cinema architecture outside London. The building, besides containing a 1,600-seater cinema, had several cafés, a ballroom, a writing room and lounges. The Elite closed as a cinema in 1977 and was used for a time as a bingo hall. It now has a new lease of life as a night-club.

A sailor and his bride leaving St Mary's Church after their wedding in 1929, with well-wishers touching his collar for luck. The band round the sailor's collar represents Nelson's great victory at Trafalgar and is therefore thought to be a good luck charm. The sailor is wearing his tropical uniform, which he is entitled to use on this occasion.

A sailor's wedding with a difference: the happy couple leaving church with the matelot's pet monkey clinging to his uniform.

May and Dorrie Stevenson on a swing in Woodthorpe Grange Park, early 1920s. These are the daughters of Frank Stevenson, the photographer of most of the pictures in this book. They appeared in many of his photographs, sometimes as the centre of attraction but often just as extras.

Children happily playing on a see-saw in Woodthorpe Grange Park, 1920s. Simple games like this are still well loved by all young people.

Local schoolgirls gathering daffodils in the small wood at the Mansfield Road end of the Forest Recreation Ground – a fragment of the great Sherwood Forest that, in the Middle Ages, stretched from Nottingham to Worksop.

Boys of the Nottingham Bluecoat School in Mansfield Road boxing in the school playground, 1930. The school was founded in 1706, moved to High Pavement in 1723 and then to Mansfield Road in 1853. This T.C. Hine building was the home of the school until 1967, when it moved to its present site in Aspley Lane. Samuel Turner, who was a pupil of the school in the early nineteenth century, became a local boxing champion and was considered to be Champion of All England at his weight.

The thirteenth-century Nottingham Castle gatehouse, 1922. This gatehouse, which embodies the last remaining part of the old castle, was in a ruinous state when in 1908 the Corporation began its restoration. This is the archway through which many kings of England rode, most famously Richard III on his way to Bosworth Field – and his death. The Norman castle was built as a frontier fortress, facing north, a fact usually overlooked by visitors admiring the view over the Trent Valley. To the Normans the outcrop of sandstone, with its sheer cliff providing a natural defence, was the obvious site for a castle. During the next six centuries the castle was the scene of much turmoil, but with the coming of the Tudors it fell into disrepair. At the end of the Civil War the castle was completely demolished and the Duke of Newcastle built a pseudo-classical mansion on the site, while retaining the old name. The last great event in the history of the castle occurred in 1831 when the Reform Bill rioters gutted the building; it remained empty for forty-five years before being converted into a museum of fine art.

King Charles Street, 1923. The name of this Georgian street commemorates the raising of the royal standard here on 22 July 1642. The standard, raised by the order of King Charles I, symbolised the commencement of the Civil War between the Royalists and the Parliamentarians. It is believed that, having originally raised the standard in the castle keep, the king then ordered the flag to be flown in the outer bailey, which then covered a much larger area. The local response was only lukewarm, and on 13 September 1642 the king and his troops moved on to Shrewsbury.

Rock carvings in The Ropewalk. These rock ornaments were carved for Alderman Thomas Herbert on one of the terraces of his garden below his house in The Ropewalk. The large vase bears the date 1839, and during the following four decades more decorative carvings were completed by Thomas Herbert and his cousin William Herbert in adjoining caves. These included statues of historical figures such as Daniel in the lions' den, John Wesley, the Duke of Wellington and Lord Nelson.

All that remained of the Nottingham Cavalry Barracks in 1921. The barracks were built in 1792 and had a resident garrison to keep the peace in the town. They were not permanently occupied after 1861 and around 1871 the majority of the buildings were pulled down.

Three painters walking down Park Steps, 1953. Park Steps is an ancient right of way leading from the town to Lenton and until 1829 was only a steep track. The Duke of Newcastle was then beginning the development of the castle park as a residential estate, and houses in The Ropewalk and Park Valley were the first to be built.

Priory Courtyard, Friar Lane, 1921. This photograph shows the rear of Dorothy Vernon's house, which was built over the remains of the Carmelite Priory established by Reginald Grey around 1271. Dorothy Vernon and her husband, John Manners of Haddon Hall, acquired the property in 1574 and lived here for five or six years – it was here that their four children were born. In the courtyard are the last remains of the priory – a few broken pillars and a sundial on a stone column. Sadly the house was demolished in a road-widening scheme in 1927.

Nottingham's smallest house, Wollaton Street, 1927. This tiny house was occupied by Harriet Woodcock, but was demolished in 1930 in the Corporation's slum clearance scheme.

Severn's Yard off Middle Pavement, 1928. The old-established Severn's Restaurant is on the left: this building was originally part of a fifteenth-century merchant's house and is one of the oldest in Nottingham. When the Broad Marsh Shopping Centre was planned Severn's was threatened with demolition, but fortunately an alternative solution was found. The whole edifice was dismantled and removed to Castle Road in 1970 where, after restoration, it became the premises of the Lace Centre.

Weekday Cross, *c.* 1930 – the site of a weekday market until 1800 and the spot where royal proclamations were made. The first cross was built for *2s 8d* around 1529 and was replaced in 1741 by a cross known as the Butcher's Cross made by Thomas Sandby. This was demolished in 1804, but a replica of the cross was built here in 1993 for £12,000.

Drury Hill, 1922. One of Frank Stevenson's and many other photographers' favourite locations, it still has fond memories for many citizens of Nottingham. Besides having a character of its own it also possessed a pungent smell, which drifted from a leather workshop. After centuries of existence this street disappeared beneath the concrete of the Broad Marsh Shopping Centre.

Trent Street, 1929. This street crosses the Nottingham Canal and replaces a wooden bridge which was a short cut to the old Midland Railway station on Station Street. Outside A.R. Atkey's motor spare parts warehouse are two splendid motor cars – the first a Wolseley and the other a Ford. On the right is one of Boots offices, originally Atkey's main premises. In the distance, beyond Canal Street, is the High Pavement Unitarian Chapel, which was opened in 1876 and contains stained-glass windows designed by Edward Burne-Jones. Following its closure as a chapel in 1980, the building was converted into a lace museum and has now become the Pitcher and Piano bar-restaurant.

*Opposite, top*: Motor barges on the Nottingham Canal, 1930. Traffic on canals was then predominantly commercial, but since its decline the huge increase in leisure craft has given the waterways a new lease of life. The Trent Navigation Warehouse has now been converted to restaurants and bars as part of the redevelopment of the area.

*Bottom*: Coalpit Lane from Hockley, 1934. Hamilton's drapery store on the left and the houses in the distance were due to be demolished in the Corporation's slum clearance programme. Hamilton's was replaced by a Montague Burton tailor's shop, and at the same time Coalpit Lane was renamed Cranbrook Street. F.W. Woolworth's store on the right was a 3*d* and 6*d* bazaar; items such as an eighteen-piece tea-set had their cups, saucers and plates individually priced.

Red Lion Street in 1933, just prior to its demolition. This street, alternatively called Narrow Marsh, was named after the Red Lion public house at the Plumptre Square end. The white building on the right is the Loggerheads public house, which is now the only building to survive.

The remaining structures on Red Lion Street, 1933. This part of the Marshes was quickly rebuilt as a small estate of council houses, but Broad Marsh remained largely undeveloped for thirty years.

The last of the back-to-back houses in Narrow Marsh. This area had the reputation of having the worst housing in Nottingham, and it was probably the first occasion on which the sun had shone on these tenements.

Workmen bricking up some of the caves that were discovered behind the houses on Red Lion Street. Many of these caves were used in the past for tanning or brewing, and have now been reopened as a tourist attraction.

The path by the River Leen at Basford, 1950. The course of the Leen from its source at Hollinwell to the River Trent is fairly short, but the river was of great importance in the past, turning water wheels and supplying the needs of the priories of Newstead and Lenton as well as Nottingham Castle.

Children fishing in the River Leen at Bobbers Mill, 1950. The river here is only shallow, but in 1947 there was serious flooding in the area when it burst its banks.

Clayton's Wharf and Bridge at Lenton, 1929. The bridge spanned the Nottingham Canal, but a new bridge was built in 1954 as the old one was unsafe for heavy loads. Trevethick's boatyard, previously Gilbert's, is on the left bank.

A winter scene at Trent Bridge, 1950. In the foreground a group of people are contemplating the view – the river almost in flood, the deserted landing stage and the darkening sky.

The Riverside Pleasure Park attendant. This man, who hired out rowing boats, fishing rods and deck-chairs, appears to have seen it all before and intends his word to be law. The park on Trent Lane, with its small beach of sand, swings, boats and other amusements, was for many children a seaside holiday-at-home.

A great character study of an old man selling copies of *Old Moore's Almanack* at the corner of Long Row and King Street. This type of itinerant has been replaced by today's purveyors of *The Big Issue*.

The Old Market Square when trolley buses and Streamline taxi-cabs were still running on Nottingham's roads, 1952.

A crowd heckling Lieutenant-Colonel John Cordeaux in the Old Market Square, 1964. These regular open-air meetings were enjoyed by all who participated.

The corner of Wheeler Gate and Friar Lane, 1960. All these buildings were to be demolished in the next two years, the seventeenth-century building of the Oriental Café being the greatest loss. The ornamental plasterwork ceiling was fortunately saved, and although intended for Newdigate House it was eventually moved to Holme Pierrepont Hall. In 1998 the plasterwork was moved again to a house in Ladbroke Square, London.

Greyfriar Gate, c. 1939. Collin's Almshouses on the right were closed in 1938 and purchased by the Nottingham Co-operative Society for £60,000, but the war prevented rebuilding on the site. During this period the almshouses were used as an air raid shelter; in 1954 the Corporation bought them and the site was eventually used as part of the Broad Marsh Shopping Centre. The Walter Fountain in the centre was another fixture until 1950, when it was demolished in a road-widening scheme.

An aerial view of the city centre from above the Meadows, 1963. In the left foreground are the railway sidings known as Spike Island, where the Inland Revenue complex has now been built. In the centre foreground the Magistrates Courts have replaced a railway goods warehouse as part of the plan to redevelop this area. Nearer the city centre a large stretch of land is being cleared in preparation for the construction of the Broad Marsh Shopping Centre. Clearly recognisable is the castle on its outcrop of rock, and beyond it is the round tower of the General Hospital.

The city centre from the north, 1969. The houses in the foreground have now been pulled down and replaced by colleges of the Nottingham Trent University. Near the centre of the photograph is the tower of the Newton Building, which opened in 1958 as the Nottingham and District Technical College, and from which the Nottingham Trent University has developed. On the left are the clock tower and the remains of the Victoria railway station before the construction of the Victoria Shopping Centre. Further away is the conspicuous dome of the Council House, and to the right are the tower blocks near Maid Marian Way.

The General Post Office in Queen Street, 1960. This was built by Thomas Fish for £95,000 and opened in 1898, but forty years later it was proposed to demolish the building and rebuild it on modern lines. The war necessitated the cancellation of this scheme, but the offices on the left became the regional headquarters of

The south front of the Nottingham High School, 1959. The school, originally known as the Free School, was founded by Dame Agnes Mellers in 1513 and was first based in St Mary's Church. After a few years it moved to Stoney Street where it remained until 1868 when the present school, designed by Simpson and Hine, was opened. The war memorial in the gardens was designed by an old boy, Colonel Brewill, and unveiled by the Duke of Portland in 1922.

the Civil Defence. In 1972 the post office moved to new premises that replaced the right-hand section of the old building. After standing empty for many years this building has been reconstructed, leaving the façade virtually unchanged.

An art class in the Nottingham High School for Girls, 1947. The school was founded in 1875, and was situated in Oxford Street until 1880 when it moved to its present home – Clarence Lodge in Arboretum Street. This was originally the house of James Hartshon, a lace manufacturer, but since that time it has been considerably enlarged.

An aerial view of Lenton and Radford, 1960. In the left foreground is Lenton Lodge, originally the gatehouse to Wollaton Hall but now completely isolated from the park. Occupying almost all the land in the centre of the photograph on each side of Triumph Road are the factories of the Raleigh Cycle Company. The firm had by this time reached the limits of its expansion in Nottingham but was continuing to expand its manufacturing operations overseas. In the distance are the Radford Gas Works and the Player's bonded warehouses, still painted in their colour of wartime grey.

The frame shop at the Raleigh Cycle Company, 1944. Although most of the firm's production capacity was then devoted to war work, utility bicycles were still being manufactured. The company evolved from a small workshop in Raleigh Street started by Woodhead, Angois and Ellis in 1886. It was only after Frank Bowden invested in the business that the firm began to expand rapidly, and in 1888 the Raleigh Cycle Company was founded.

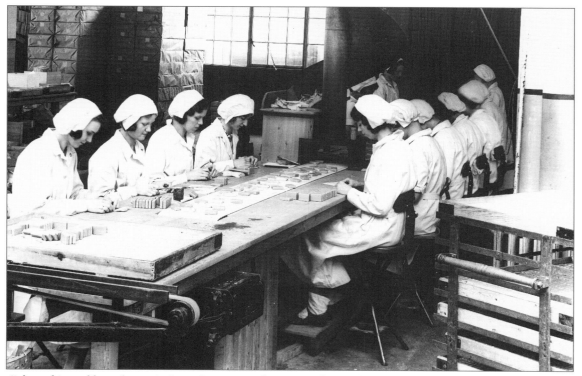

Girls packing tablets of soap in Boots Beeston works, 1928. This packing line was fairly primitive, but in 1933 the new D.10 site was opened and was immediately hailed as a wonder factory.

Trent Bridge from the air, 1946. The unfinished County Hall is in the left foreground: building commenced in 1938 but virtually ceased in 1941. After the end of the Second World War construction continued in a very desultory fashion, but in 1954 a new block and a seventeen-storey clock tower were planned. The tower was never completed as the land was considered unsuitable for such a building. The County Hall was finished in 1965, by which time Lovers' Walk on the river bank had been removed. Trent Bridge cricket ground and the Nottingham Forest and Notts. County football grounds are plainly visible to the right: these were the days before huge sports stadiums were constructed. On the far bank of the River Trent is Turney's Leather Works which, following its closure in 1981, has been converted into apartments.

The flooded Colliery Road by the River Trent, March 1947. These floods were caused by heavy snowfalls in January and February of that year followed in March by torrential rain. Coal production was halted at Clifton Colliery and miners had to go to Greyfriars Hall in Greyfriars Gate to collect their wages. The colliery finally closed in 1969; North Wilford Power Station beyond, which was opened in 1925, continued generating electricity until 1981.

Workman catching fish while cleaning the pond in the Victoria Embankment Memorial Gardens, 1964. The gardens were laid out in 1927 on land given by Sir Jesse Boot for use as a memorial park. The Memorial Arch in the background, designed by T. Wallis Gordon, was unveiled in November 1927.

A wintry scene at the junction of Derby Road and Clifton Boulevard, 1958. The city ring road here was the outer limit of city trolley bus routes, and service number 45, which ran from Trent Bridge to Middleton Boulevard, was in 1962 the first to be converted to motor buses.

A study in light and shade: the gateway to St Mary's Church at Wollaton Park. This church, which was designed by T. Cecil Howitt, was built between 1937 and 1939, and was endowed by William G. Player who, before moving to Whatton Manor, lived at Lenton Hirst on Adams Hill.

A young family leaving the Arboretum one sunny morning in 1948. To give the citizens of Nottingham an opportunity to relax in a scenic park was the original idea behind the creation of the Arboretum. However, for the first few years after its opening in 1852 the public were admitted free on only three days a week, while there was an admission charge of 6*d* for adults and 3*d* for children on other days.

War memorials in St Mary's Church. The memorial on the left is to the men of the South Notts. Hussars and the one on the right is to the men of the three Robin Hood battalions of the Sherwood Foresters. The church has presided over Nottingham for centuries, and is a cathedral in all but name. The greater part of the present building was erected in the fifteenth century with money provided by wealthy merchants. In 1839 it was discovered that the tower was unsafe and needed complete renovation. A proposal was made that the church should be demolished, but fortunately that proposition was defeated and Sir Gilbert Scott and William Moffatt completed the restoration.

A man with a marathon task, cutting the grass with hand shears round the graves and headstones in St Nicholas' churchyard.

The procession of the Lord Mayor and his officers from St Mary's Church after the Nottingham High School Founder's Day Service, 1964. Dame Agnes Mellers, who founded the school in 1513, ordered a service to be held annually on 16 June, the Feast of the Translation of St Richard – her husband's name day. The Founder's Day service is now held on the nearest Saturday to 16 June and is followed by a bread, ale and cheese ceremony in the Council House. The original endowment for the feast was £1, and after the purchase of the food and drink the residue was given to the poorest scholar to pray for the souls of Agnes and Richard Mellers. The distribution is now given to the youngest scholar in the school. The ceremony was revived in 1923 after a lapse of several centuries and, with the exception of the Goose Fair, is the most ancient ritual in Nottingham.

The almost deserted platforms of the Victoria railway station in 1960 – during the last decade of its existence. The major railway stations built at the end of the nineteenth century, with their cathedral-like proportions, were made to impress. This station had a unique atmosphere, one which the Midland Railway station does not possess, and this photograph of the sunlight pouring through the glass roof captures it well.

Victoria railway station, 1964. A train has just disappeared into the Mansfield Road tunnel and is emitting smoke into the grimy atmosphere. The station was difficult to run, as there were bottlenecks at both north and south ends. On the left is a 50-ft diameter turntable, which could be used either hydraulically or manually.

Another study of sunshine and shadow at Victoria railway station. The station was opened without ceremony on 24 May 1900 and for nearly seventy years graced Milton Street, being built largely of Darley Dale stone and Nottingham brick. The last passenger service left Victoria station on 2 September 1967, although goods trains continued to run through the station until May 1968.

A train passing Lenton South Junction, 1929. The locomotive No. 408 is an LMS 4–4–0 class 2P designed by Samuel Johnson in the 1890s and rebuilt by Henry Fowler between 1910 and 1920. It bears the headlamp code for an express passenger or newspaper train. On the skyline beyond, Nottingham Castle can be seen.

A nondescript local train on the Midland Railway, passing Trent Lane signal gantry on its way into Nottingham, 1914.

Members of the Nottingham branch of the Railway Correspondence and Travel Society on an excursion to Crewe, 1955. Unfortunately this was a rainy day, but everyone seems to be full of enthusiasm.

The East Midlander excursion train making an impressive picture on its outing to Crewe in 1955. The locomotive is No. 61554, a class B12/3 redesign by Nigel Gresley of a Great Eastern Railway design by S.D. Holden. On the right is an old-style telegraph post.

Two dirty locomotives at the south end of Victoria railway station billowing out clouds of smoke and steam, 1950s. This was a common sight then, and although the engines are of pre-war vintage there is still an air of romance attached to them.

# *The Vale of Belvoir and the Wolds*

The market cross in Colston Bassett, 1929. This cross was, in 1933, the first National Trust acquisition in the county, although the base is still owned by Nottinghamshire County Council. The original cross was erected by Ralph Bassett when he obtained permission in 1257 from Henry III to hold a weekly market here and a fair on the Eve of St Faith. The cross was reconstructed on the old base in 1831 to commemorate the coronation of William IV.

Car Colston, 1931. This peaceful village scattered round the largest green in the county cannot have changed greatly since Dr Robert Thoroton, the historian, lived here in the seventeenth century. At the far end of the village, beyond St Mary's Church, is a second, smaller green, and there were gates at the three exits to the village to prevent animals straying.

A Screveton lane, 1929. The house on the right is White House Farm, then owned by Thomas Marsh: his daughter is in the front garden working hard at lime-washing the walls of the farmhouse. The farm has been run by the Marsh family for generations and is now owned by Phillip Thoroton Marsh. John Knight is driving the pony and trap from the direction of the Royal Oak Inn.

The Georgian south front of Staunton Hall, 1889. The Staunton family have lived on the same estate since the eleventh century – a claim few other families can make. The present house dates from the sixteenth century and bears the scars of the Civil War, when it was attacked by the Parliamentarians. During the eighteenth century various changes and additions were made to this delightful house. Traditionally, the head of the Staunton family presents the golden key of the Staunton Tower at Belvoir Castle to the visiting sovereign to open the great door of the tower.

A bicycling party outside Staunton Hall, 1905. The Revd Harvey Staunton, in the centre, played cricket for the county; tragically he died in Mesopotamia in the First World War. His sister Beatrice is on the far left and his brother George, who succeeded as the squire, is on the right. George Staunton was in turn succeeded in 1965 by the present squire, Edmund Staunton.

The largely unaltered village of Scarrington with its few wide streets. The church of St John has a fourteenth-century spire, but a large part of the church was rebuilt in the 1860s. The huge pile of horseshoes built outside the old smithy has become a local attraction.

Two primitively carved ships' figureheads outside a farmhouse at Car Hill, Scarrington, 1931. These were brought here by Mr Nethercliffe, a mariner, who then renamed the house Mermaid Cottage; prior to this it was called Ebenezer Cottage. Sadly the subsequent owners of the cottage removed the figureheads and they ended their existence in the field behind the house. Carved figureheads were intended to bring good fortune and represented the spirit of the ship, and it was considered bad luck if the figurehead was cut off or damaged.

A hive of activity in a farmyard in Aslockton, 1928. These steam-powered threshing machines were labour-intensive and extremely noisy. Every man was continuously occupied: the steam engine had to be fed with coal, the boiler replenished with water from the urns in the foreground, the grain bagged and the bales of straw stacked.

The Butter Cross in Bingham Market Place, on a sunny day in 1950. The right to hold a market here was granted in 1314, but lapsed in about 1900 and was revived in 1975. The cross was designed by T.C. Hine and built in 1861 in memory of John Hassall, the late agent to the Earl of Chesterfield, then lord of the manor.

A corner of Bingham Market Place, 1950. Doncaster's drapery shop in the centre had already been established for over a hundred years, and on the far right Marsden's grocery shop was one of a chain of local shops that, like Lipton's, Meadow Dairy, Maypole and Home & Colonial, were to close as supermarkets became popular.

Whatton Manor, 1932. The gardens were open on this occasion for the benefit of the Queen's Institute of District Nursing. The house was built in 1838–40 by Anthony Salvin, the designer of Harlaxton Manor and Thoresby Hall, for Thomas Dickinson Hall. In 1928 William G. Player, the son of John Player, bought the house, which in 1962 was demolished. A Georgian-style house was then built nearby; this is still occupied by the Player family.

The Griffin's Head, Whatton-in-the-Vale, 1928. The Nottingham to Grantham road ran past this inn, which was owned by William Swingler who was also a local farmer. The village has now been bypassed, and after the inn was demolished in 1996 a small housing estate known as Griffin's End was built on the land.

A Sunday school class outside Tythby Church, 1907. In the centre is Miss Chaworth-Musters from the nearby Wiverton Hall. All the boys have wing collars and the girls are wearing smock dresses and boots. The church of Holy Trinity is full of Georgian furnishings, including a double-decker pulpit, the squire's pew and box pews.

The main street of Cropwell Bishop, 1930. In the background is the fifteenth-century tower of St Giles' Church. When the old Colston Bassett church was replaced by the present building in 1892, the pews and pulpit were transferred here. On the right is the old schoolhouse, built in 1877 and now the Youth and Community Centre.

Wiverton Hall, 1920. This is the north front of the nineteenth-century hall, which contains part of the Tudor gatehouse of the old home of the Chaworth family. During the Civil War the house, which was garrisoned by Lord John Chaworth, was visited by Queen Henrietta Maria and also Prince Rupert after his famous quarrel with Charles I. After storming Shelford Manor in November 1645 Major-General Poyntz marched on Wiverton Hall, which was forced to surrender. After the Parliamentarians had secured the house it was almost completely demolished.

A fifteenth-century doorway in the old gatehouse, Wiverton Hall. This gives a glimpse of the winding stairway that, since the alterations made to the house in the nineteenth century, serves only to give access to the lead roof.

Admiring onlookers and one policeman watch the Belvoir Hunt, led by William Biston, the first whipper-in, move off from Colston Bassett on New Year's Day, 1938. Behind the dogs is the huntsman, George Tonge, followed by the two Masters of the Belvoir Hunt – at that time, Lord Daresbury and Colonel F.G.D. Colman. The history of the Belvoir Hunt extends back to the seventeenth century, and to tell its story is to relate the rise of fox-hunting in this country.

High summer in the Vale of Belvoir: the view from Owthorpe Hill, 1950s. The hamlet at the foot of the hill, which comprises only a farm or two and a few cottages, is still unchanged.

Owthorpe Church, 1932. This tiny church, which stands in the middle of a field, was partly rebuilt in 1705. Inside is the monument to Colonel John Hutchinson, the Puritan commander of Nottingham Castle during the Civil War. Owthorpe Hall, his home, was destroyed by the Royalists during the war and, although rebuilt by the colonel, was demolished in the nineteenth century.

All Saints' Church, Cotgrave, 1932. This fourteenth-century church was unfortunately gutted in 1996 when it was set alight by vandals. However, eighteen months later the church was reopened for services, having been completely restored. The Manvers Arms on the left, which was built in about 1725, was originally a coaching inn known as the Black Lion.

A quiet corner of Cotgrave, 1932. A photographer would nowadays risk his life to take this picture at the junction of Main Street and Candleby Lane.

A horse pulling a wagon overloaded with hay from a field near Plumtree – a classic scene of country life and now only a memory.

Men forking hay on to stacks in a Cotgrave farmyard. Frank Stevenson's talent was to produce a memorable photograph from an ordinary scene, and although it may have been posed it still appeared spontaneous.

A farmworker with a scythe taking a rest in a field of oats near Keyworth. Harvesting with a scythe is a centuries-old craft that is now almost extinct.

*Opposite, top*: Plumtree Smithy, 1929. James Barnet (right) and John Hodgett are bending a hoop in the smithy on the Main Road. After the closure of the smithy, a house which incorporates the arch in its façade was built on the site.

*Bottom*: The remains of Plumtree windmill, 1929. The mill was already derelict when, during the First World War, it was the target of an arson attack by youths who were incensed at being fined for rowdyism by Mr Turner, the local magistrate who owned the mill. Nothing now remains of it.

The Red Heart, Easthorpe Street, Ruddington, with a group of schoolgirls passing the inn, 1930. This was originally a sixteenth-century farmhouse and was later given a licence to brew and sell ale. Legends relate the stories of two ghosts who haunt the inn – one a soldier of Cromwell's army and the other a little girl who died here in a fire.

A group of farm workers outside the Red Heart, Ruddington, having a lark with Charlie Attewell, the village lamplighter, climbing a ladder to nowhere.

A moment from bygone childhood: a group of children playing round the village pump in the centre of Gotham, 1925. Until around 1820 there was a large elm tree on this site, and one of the tales of Gotham refers to the local people having only one knife between them: this was stuck in the tree for their common use. Earl Howe presented the village with this pump, which drew water from springs rising in nearby hills. Pumps were the only source of water for the inhabitants of Gotham until 1933, when the village was connected to Nottingham's water system. This village pump has now been completely rebuilt to a similar design, with seats inside the railings.

The spire of Bradmore Church appearing above old cottages in the centre of the village. The tower and spire are the only parts of the medieval church, which survived a disastrous fire in 1706 that destroyed most of the village. Sir Thomas Parkyns of nearby Bunny Hall rebuilt the village, but not the church. In 1881 a small mission hall was built on to the tower, and services are still held there.

The Rancliffe Arms, Bunny, 1928. This timber-framed inn was the venue from 1712 to 1810 of the annual wrestling contest begun by Sir Thomas Parkyns. The first prize was a gold laced hat, value 22s, and the second prize was 3s. Wrestling was the squire's greatest passion, and he wrote a book on the subject entitled *The Cornish Hugg Wrestler*.

Children congregated outside the old village school, Bunny, 1932. The school was designed in 1700 by Sir Thomas Parkyns, who was also responsible for the construction of most of the village. The plaque above the door is inscribed with the rules of entry to the school. Children of parents who contributed to public levies were charged 6*d* quarterly and others were admitted free. At the rear of the school were four rooms for four poor widows, endowed by Lady Anne Parkyns, who also provided gowns and petticoats for each widow every other year.

Boys clustered round one of their friends mending a bicycle in Church Street, Bunny – all probably hoping for a ride after the repair. The two nearest cottages have now been pulled down and replaced with new houses.

Widmerpool Hall, 1926. This Elizabethan-style hall was built in 1872–3 for Major George Robertson by Henry Clutton. Major Robertson was a descendant of George Robinson (the family varied the spelling of their name), who built a number of watermills on the River Leen in the eighteenth century. The hall is now the Automobile Association training centre.

A farm-hand collecting water from the village pond in Rempstone to take to a nearby farm. The cottage, one of the two oldest in the village, later housed the village post office; it has now been well restored and is Grade II listed. The water tank is still in use, supplying water to steam engines at Rempstone Steam and Craft Fair.

The main street at East Leake, 1929. The church is early-English but was largely restored in 1886. The cottages on the right have now been demolished; the bakery on the left is, however, still standing. A stream runs behind the old bakery, and that part of the village still retains an old-fashioned atmosphere.

A man strolling along a tree-lined lane near Stanford-on-Soar. The meadows here have always been liable to flooding from the nearby River Soar, but the river is a great attraction for fishermen and picnickers.

A girl at Sutton Bonington in 1955, holding two three-day-old kids who are finding life good.

# Along the Trent

Beeston Lock, 1956. This very attractive lock with white-rendered lock-keepers' houses in the background has an unusual lock system. Here there are locks at right angles to each other, allowing boats to enter the Trent both above and below Beeston Weir.

An old road-mender preparing for his day's work outside his cottage at Ratcliffe-on-Soar, 1919. Many country roads were still only tracks and local parish councils were obliged to use old methods of repair.

An Automobile Association patrolman coming to the aid of a woman driver at Ratcliffe-on-Soar, 1955. The salute from an AA or RAC patrolman as he passed by is a courtesy which has vanished from the roads – like this motor-cycle combination.

84

The lock-keepers' houses at Redhill Lock, Ratcliffe-on-Soar, 1918. These isolated houses still exist, although the lock has been changed to a flood lock since the flood improvement scheme of 1986–8 on the River Soar.

Redhill Lock, Ratcliffe-on-Soar, 1931. The old hump-backed bridge still remains but the wooden towing bridge has disappeared. This stretch of the River Soar, which is dominated by the nearby power station, has now become an attractive marina.

Thrumpton Hall, 1931. This house, built in the seventeenth century by Gervase Pigot and his son, also named Gervase, incorporates the remains of an earlier house. The previous owners were the Powdrills who were concerned in the Gunpowder Plot. They concealed Father Garnett, one of the leading conspirators, in the priest's hole that lies at the foot of a secret staircase built in the thickness of a chimney breast.

The magnificent staircase, from the Restoration period, at Thrumpton Hall. This cantilevered staircase adorned with acanthus scrolls rises to the top of the house, and is considered to be the finest in the county.

Clifton Hall, 1929. Built between 1778 and
1797 by John Carr on the site of an earlier
house, this was the home of the Clifton family
until 1958. The house has a Page's Room with
historic wood panel paintings, and until its
closure as a private house the conservatory
contained an aviary of canaries. After the sale of
the house a girls' school was built in the grounds,
and in 1976 the Trent Polytechnic, now the
Nottingham Trent University, opened here.

One of the fine carved monuments to the Clifton
family in St Mary's Church, Clifton. This one
commemorates Sir Gervase Clifton who died in
1587. 'Gervase the Gentle', as he was known,
wears a ruff and Elizabethan armour, and his
two wives lie beside him – one on each side.

Farmworkers stacking barley on Plowright's Farm at Barton-in-Fabis, 1930. Roman remains are frequently found in the fields here: two mosaic floors were found near the hills on the left. The Ratcliffe-on-Soar power station, which was built in the early 1960s, now dominates the skyline to the right.

The TIL house in Clifton, 1950s. This is named after Thomas Lambert who, in 1707, refaced the original fourteenth-century wattle and daub cottage with brick and added a wing to the house. In 1994, when the house was in a ruinous condition, a Nottingham couple bought it, and it has now been restored to its former glory.

A cart loaded with hay on the Nottingham Road at Clifton on a frosty November day, 1922. The thatched cottage on the left stands at the corner of Glapton Lane, surrounded by a group of tall trees, which, like the cottage itself, has now gone.

A knife-grinder in Clifton, 1921. This old man who travelled the road with his horse and dog is a source of fascination to these children, who have stopped their games to watch him. Today this trade would probably only be seen at a craft fair or a theme park.

Muck-spreading on a farm at Clifton, 1926. On the left with a sack round his waist is Bill Swain, and on the right is Harry Mann, the farmer. The hamlet of Glapton is in the middle distance. All this land is now part of the Clifton housing estate, which was developed between 1951 and 1973.

Glapton Lane, Clifton, 1928. The hamlet of Glapton, although part of the village of Clifton, was separated from it by the main road into Nottingham. The double-gabled house, built in 1899, was owned by Harry Mann (pictured above) who farmed nearby, and the farm building in the foreground was part of William Beecroft's farm. The house is now the only building remaining of the old hamlet of Glapton.

The bridge over Fairham Brook at the beginning of the walk to Clifton Grove, 1933. In the background is the Round House, which was a tea house on the Clifton Hall estate. One of the pleasures for Nottingham people in the past was to cross the River Trent and walk along Clifton Grove, and either picnic or have tea at Clifton. This bridge and folly were demolished when the construction of Clifton Bridge began in 1954.

Main Road, Wilford, when the village still had a rural atmosphere, 1924. The first three cottages on the right have now been demolished, and the remainder are derelict. On the far right is the old Manor House in which Henry Kirke White, the poet, is believed to have stayed.

Henry Ireton's house in Attenborough, 1930. Ireton was born in this house in 1611 and served as a major-general under Cromwell in the Civil War. He was a member of the court that tried Charles I, and in 1649 signed the king's death warrant. When Ireton died of the plague in 1651 he was buried in Westminster Abbey, but after the Restoration his body, with that of Cromwell, was put on display on the gallows at Tyburn.

West Bridgford Hall, 1930. The hall was built in 1768–74 by Mundy Musters and John Musters, and in the nineteenth century became the home of the Heymann family. In 1923 the hall became the offices of West Bridgford Urban District Council.

Youngsters sliding on the frozen Grantham Canal, winter 1963. The canal was closed to traffic in 1936, and although some stretches of it have recently been cleared, this part – in West Bridgford – is now rather overgrown.

Holme Pierrepont Hall, 1932. The old home of the Pierrepont family, it still belongs to descendants of the original builder. The earliest surviving part of the house is the Tudor frontage, which was rendered in 1810. The rendering and the ivy were removed in 1970–2, revealing again the delightful red Norfolk bricks.

A Civil Defence exercise in Colwick Park, 1940. This was a full-scale trial for all the civilian, military and local authority services, and realistic bomb damage and injuries were simulated. Here, members of the Women's Voluntary Service are preparing field kitchens with a pall of smoke drifting over them.

Colwick Junction carnival queen Betty Hardy is crowned by the retiring queen Ann Brown at the Whitsuntide carnival, 1958.

Boys fishing at Burton Joyce, 1960. The river flows in a great curve towards Burton Joyce and is only a short walk from the Nottingham Road. Sunday School outings and family picnics to this stretch of the river were once regular treats.

A tug pulling a string of barges beneath the cliffs at Radcliffe-on-Trent, 1927. The period between the two world wars was the time when commercial river and canal traffic reached its peak, and when Nottingham for a few years could seriously claim to be an inland port.

The Kinema at Radcliffe-on-Trent, 1932. The building was constructed in 1870 as the village school and was used as such until 1909 when it became a cinema. This was known as the Picture House, and serial films were shown on Saturday mornings – 2d at the front and 4d at the back. In the 1950s the cinema, then known as the Rex, was bought by the parish council to be used as a village hall, although films were still shown once or twice a week into the 1960s.

The Manvers Arms, Radcliffe-on-Trent, 1928. The women on the right seem to be plucking up courage either to use the weighing machine or to enter the public house. The inn, originally called the White Hart, was designed by William Wilkins in the early nineteenth century for the Earl of Manvers.

Water Lane, Radcliffe-on-Trent, 1925. The shuttered building is Smith's fish and chip shop, which was the original Co-operative Society butcher's shop. The open-fronted building is Harrison's, corn merchants, and next door are their shop premises. All these buildings were demolished in 1963 when Hamelin's factory was built.

John Cragg's clog shop at the corner of Water Lane and Mount Pleasant, Radcliffe-on-Trent, 1925. This later became a fish and chip shop run by Tommy 'Tonic' Tinkler. Although named Mount Pleasant on the maps of the time, this lane, with the narrowest pavement and with washing hanging across it, was called Knight's Hill by the villagers, after Florence Knight who had a general shop at the top end of the street.

A farmer working his horses in a field near the disused Newton Windmill, 1929. This mill, which it is believed once stood on the Forest in Nottingham, was in use until about 1918, when the miller was Walter Harrison.

The corn harvest being tied in sheaves in a field next to the now dilapidated Newton Windmill, 1936. The mill was dismantled in the 1950s, but the stone base, which belongs to the Crown, has been renovated.

Harvest-time on a Shelford farm. The farm worker, in belt and braces and leading his horse, is perhaps unfairly our idea of a countryman in the early part of the twentieth century.

Frank Stevenson on the left and Harold Caunton mending a bicycle tyre puncture at Shelford, 1912. This was a common occurrence for cyclists in those days, although the rough land here was an additional hazard.

Caythorpe Mill, 1927. This mill, built in about 1745, is one of the six water mills originally on the Dover Beck. Known locally as Gregory's Mill, this was still in operation until 1953. Well restored, with its wheel still in place, the building is now a pottery, with the mill storerooms converted into a house.

Cattle grazing along the bank of the old River Trent near Staythorpe. At Averham Weir the Trent divides, and this smaller channel follows the original course through Newark. This stretch of the river is dominated by the power stations designed by T. Cecil Howitt between 1946 and 1962. These were the beginning of a new generation of monumental power stations that were to be built in the next thirty years.

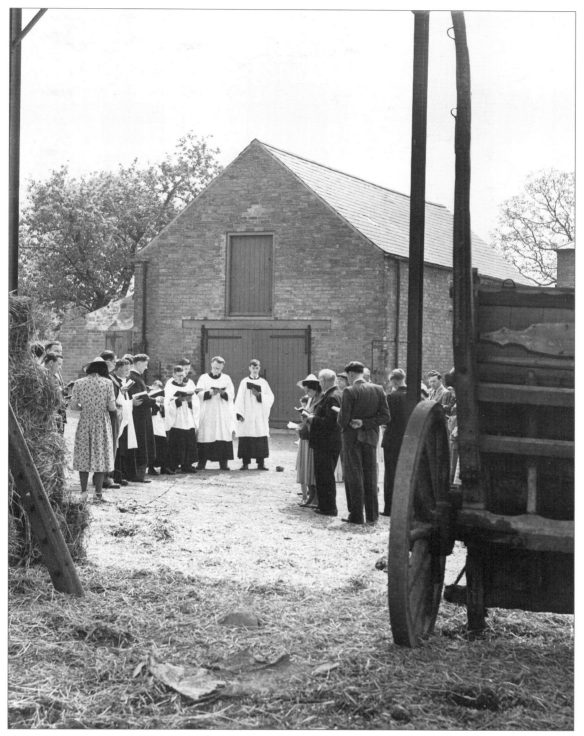

A farmyard Rogation service near Kelham, 1956. The tradition of holding this Ascension Week service has now died out.

The smithy at Carlton-on-Trent, 1922. The sign over the entrance is a rhyme: 'Gentlemen as you pass by, upon this shoe cast an eye, if it be too straight I'll make it wider, I'll ease the horse and please the rider, if lame from shoeing, as they often are, you may have them eased with the greatest care'. The smithy continued in use until 1940, when Frederick Naylor was the owner. The building has now been converted into a house, with the old arch still visible.

A hay cart in Arnold's Farm at Carlton-on-Trent, 1922. St Mary's Church, across the field, was built by brothers John and James Vere in 1851 and incorporates the twelfth-century door of the earlier church. The small extension to the cottage on the right is the village post office.

The main street at Carlton-on-Trent, 1922. The house on the far right was owned by Frank Arnold, who farmed the fields behind the church. The next building was the village school, which is now a community centre. This street was the old Great North Road, which has now been bypassed twice.

Children leaving the village school at a run in Sutton-on-Trent, 1930. In contrast is the sedate family on the right, who appear to be waiting for a bus.

The two daughters of Frank Stevenson, May and Dorrie, picking flowers in a field near Sutton-on-Trent. This charming picture of girls at play has one innocently showing her stocking suspenders.

# Newark-on-Trent
# and Mansfield

Trent Bridge, Newark, 1928. On the far bank on the left is the Ossington Coffee House, commissioned in 1882 by the temperance reformer Viscountess Ossington, daughter of the 4th Duke of Portland. The building included a coffee room, billiard room, ladies' room and bedrooms for travellers, but was never very successful. During the Second World War it was used as a billet for RAF personnel, and is now an hotel.

Two lock workers taking a break at the Town Lock, Newark, 1954. In the background is the lock-keeper's cottage.

The lock-keeper manually opening the gates of the Town Lock, Newark, 1954. The gates are now electrically powered, this being one of the busiest locks on the River Trent.

A dredging barge approaching Newark Castle, 1931. The castle was built around 1135 by Alexander the Magnificent, Bishop of Lincoln, replacing an earlier wooden fortress. In 1139 the prelate engaged in an insurrection against King Stephen, was taken prisoner and was sent to his own castle at Newark where he was compelled to purchase his liberty by the surrender to the Crown of this castle and other fortresses.

The River Trent, Newark, 1931. The period between the two world wars was almost the final chapter in the story of commercial traffic on the Trent Navigation.

The towing bridge over the River Trent in Newark, 1950. In the background are the remains of the riverside curtain wall of the castle, which was reconstructed in the fifteenth century. The greater part of the castle was demolished in 1646 at the end of the Civil War when it had been a Royalist stronghold. A cattle market, which began here in about 1839, was removed from the castle in 1886, and pleasure gardens were then laid out within the castle walls.

An unusual view of the Elbow Bridge over the River Trent in Newark, 1954. There is some dispute over the name of the river that flows through Newark. This branch of the Trent is sometimes called the Trent Navigation or the Cut, or alternatively the Devon after the minor tributary that joins the Trent upstream of the town.

An odd-looking house on the quayside at Newark, which was originally a public house named the Swan and Salmon and has now been re-opened under the same name. The Corn Exchange on the left, which has its frontage on Castle Gate, closed in 1978 and has now been converted into a night-club and a bar.

A barge passing under Trent Bridge, Newark, 1950. After a lock was constructed on the river in the late eighteenth century, Newark became an important inland port. Enlargement of the lock took place in 1831 and again in 1906, and a second lock was opened in 1952.

Market Place, Newark, 1931. This is one of the finest examples of the traditional market place in the country. Towering over it is the church of St Mary Magdalene, while in the centre of the row of buildings is the Moot Hall, built in 1708 and rebuilt in similar style in 1967. Among the businesses are Curry's the cycle company, Phillips the rope-makers, Coyne's music shop and Piper's Penny Bazaar.

The Queen's Head, Market Place, Newark, 1931. This sixteenth-century inn was restored in 1960 but still retains its characteristic Tudor frontage. The building on the right is the former Newark Stock Library, built in about 1830 by William Fowler.

Bainbridge's drapery store, Market Place, Newark, 1929. This was originally the White Hart Inn, which dates back to the fifteenth century; this timber-framed building has an even older structure behind the frontage, which is adorned with plaster saints. In 1867 John Bainbridge, draper and funeral furnisher, acquired the building for use as a shop with a sewing room on the top floor. The Nottingham Building Society bought the property in 1978 and the building has been sympathetically restored.

Balderton Gate, Newark, 1929. This street, which was once the road to London, still retains many old buildings particularly on this stretch of the road. Robb's butcher's shop on the left is still trading after nearly a century of business.

Kirkgate, Newark, 1929. The parish church dominates this old curved street, which contains buildings almost as old as the church itself. The building on the right is fifteenth-century, but has now been demolished. The church is mainly fifteenth-century but the spire, 237 ft high, dates from the fourteenth century and is a landmark for miles around Newark. The tower to the left of the church is Watson Fothergill's Nottingham and Notts. Bank, built in 1887. This distinctive building is now the Newark School of Violin Making. The ornate tower was reduced in height in 1957.

Queen Henrietta Maria's Lodging House in Kirkgate, Newark, 1931. This house is so-called because it is believed that Henrietta, wife of Charles I, stayed here during the Civil War. The house was then occupied by Lady Leeke, wife of the Royalist Colonel Leeke who was later killed leading an attack at Balderton. These were originally two separate houses of quite different design; the smaller house on the left is a relic of the twelfth-century St Leonard's Hospital and contains a fine wall drawing of a horse.

The Governor's House in Stodman Street, Newark, 1931. This was the headquarters of Sir Richard Willis, the military governor during the Civil War, and the house in which Prince Rupert was staying when Charles I reprimanded him for surrendering the port of Bristol to the enemy. The prince was then banished from the king's presence and lost his rank as a general. The tobacconist, J.E. Thompson, is using the house's connection to advertise 'Ye Olde Governor's Tobacco'.

The White Hart Yard, Newark, 1931. This could well be a scene from an earlier century. When this photograph was taken the White Hart occupied only the right-hand section of these buildings. In the days when it was a coaching inn, this yard would have been bustling with activity when the coaches from London or York pulled in. This was also the venue for cock fights and similar sporting contests; in the eighteenth century the prize was 2 guineas a battle. These buildings have now been renovated and converted into shops and cafés. A similar photograph could not be taken today as this view is blocked by a new building in the foreground.

The Ram Hotel in Castle Gate, Newark, 1931. George Eliot, the author, stayed here in 1868 and 'admired the view of the ruined castle and the quiet landscapes of the Trent'. The hotel, which is on the site of an earlier building, was in 1994, for some unaccountable reason, renamed Ye Olde Market. The adjoining Royal Oak is an even older inn: a deed of 1640 indicates that the property was given by the Earl of Exeter's widow to the St Leonard's Charities.

The old Magnus Grammar School in Appleton Gate, Newark, 1929. The school was founded in 1529 by Thomas Magnus and numbered among its pupils the musician Thomas Blow. During the Civil War the Tudor Hall was the council chamber of the governor and his officers. A new school was opened off London Road in 1909; this building is now used for meetings and as a museum.

The visit of King George V and Queen Mary to Mansfield, June 1914. The royal Daimler is being driven through huge crowds in the market place, after a welcoming ceremony at the town hall. Within two months of this event the First World War had begun, and the militia lining the route were sent to France.

The monument to Lord George Bentinck in the Market Place, Mansfield, 1930. This Gothic memorial to the younger son of the 4th Duke of Portland was designed by T.C. Hine and was originally planned with a statue in the arcaded centre section, but this idea was abandoned.

The Centre Tree in Westgate, Mansfield, 1930. This lone tree was the legendary centre of Sherwood Forest, but was felled in 1940 when it was thought to be a traffic hazard. A young oak tree was planted in the same position in 1988.

The Butter Cross in Westgate, Mansfield, 1932. This old cross is the place where, in the past, public proclamations were made and where on market days farmers' wives would bring dairy produce to sell.

The yard of the Eclipse Hotel, Westgate, Mansfield, 1930. The Swainmote Dinner, a court held three times a year before verderers (forest officers having charge of plants and venison in Sherwood Forest) took place at the Eclipse in earlier days.

Ye Olde Ramme Inn, Church Street, Mansfield, 1930. A plaque bears the date 1777, but parts of the inn are seventeenth-century. The inn, which is reputedly haunted by monks, originally had plain stucco walls but was given a mock-Tudor frontage by Mansfield Brewery.

# Sherwood Forest

A woodland scene near Edwinstowe. This area now has way-marked walks and bridleways through the ancient woodland, and although Robin Hood is perhaps only a legend, one comes closest to him here.

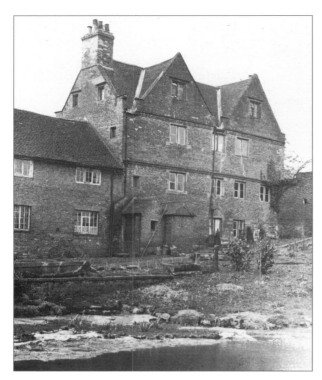

Bramcote Manor House, *c.* 1930. This early Jacobean mansion was built by the Hanley family, the donor of Hanley's Almshouses in Stoney Street, and later in Hanley Street. Originally a farmhouse in a secluded part of Bramcote, it has the reputation for being one of the best brick houses in the county. The smaller building on the left, a later addition, was demolished in the 1930s.

The south front of Bramcote Manor, 1950. Tradition says that the eighteenth-century wrought-iron balustrade was brought from a castle in France. On the right is a buttress built when the adjoining house was demolished; this itself has now been removed.

The entrance gateway framing the steps and front door of Bramcote Manor. The Bramcote estate passed from the Hanley family through several owners, until the current owner purchased the house in 1975 and restored it to its original splendour.

Main Street, Cossall, 1931. This village appears as Cossethay in D.H. Lawrence's *The Rainbow*, and the character of Ursula Brangwen is based on Louisa Burrows who lived in Church Cottage on the left.

Willoughby Almshouses in Cossall. These were founded in 1685 by George Willoughby for four poor men and four poor women. The former had a weekly allowance of *7s 6d* and the latter *6s*, plus coal – and a grey cloth gown was allowed every two years. If the inmates refused to wear the gown or were disorderly, they were removed.

Kimberley Road, Nuthall, 1923. The first house on the left was originally a farmhouse and later the Goat's Head Inn. After the inn's closure the premises were occupied by Ann Cherrington, a butcher. The next four houses are nineteenth-century properties, followed by the Horse and Groom – the stone wall of which is now all that remains. In the foreground is a passing-place section of the Nottingham to Ripley tramway.

A ploughman's lunch: a farmworker and his horse enjoying a rest at a farm near Nuthall.

Tithe houses in Brewery Street, Kimberley, 1923. These were converted from a tithe barn in the nineteenth century and later extended with brick and slate additions. In 1936 the properties were condemned by the local council and demolished. The chimney beyond the cottages is the flue from Hanson's Brewery, which in 1930 merged with the rival Hardy's Brewery, to form Hardys and Hansons Ltd.

The remains of Greasley Castle, incorporated within an eighteenth-century farmhouse. This was a fortified manor house, built by Sir Nicholas de Cantelupe around 1341, who founded the nearby Carthusian monastery of Beauvale Priory. In the background is St Mary's Church, Greasley, which contains stained glass roundels from the priory.

The ruins of Beauvale Priory, 1930. The priory was founded in 1343 by Sir Nicholas de Cantelupe under strict Carthusian rules, for twelve monks and a prior. The remains still standing, which are now heavily shored up by timbers, are the prior's house – complete with a window frame.

Abbey Farm, built adjoining the prior's house at Beauvale Priory. The farm is mainly constructed with the red sandstone blocks that were originally used in the building of the priory.

The Top Cross, Linby, 1932. The pretty colliery village of Linby, with a stream flowing down each side of the main road, has a cross at each end of the village. This cross has medieval steps, with a shaft constructed in 1869 by Montague Armiger. In 1964 the cross was damaged by vandals, but it was restored a year later. Behind the cross, Langford's butcher's boy is passing the time of day with a wagoner.

The Bottom Cross, Linby, 1932. This cross was built around 1660 to celebrate the return of the monarchy. The village of stone-built cottages still retains much of its picturesque charm. These boys are anticipating the pleasure of a drink of cream soda or possibly cherryade.

Castle Mill, Linby, 1928. This was built around 1777 by George Robinson, whose family at one time owned eight mills on the River Leen. The mill ceased operating in 1830 when all the machinery was put up for auction. In 1919 the Hucknall Torkard Co-operative Society bought the building, and closed it two years later.

The rear of Castle Mill, Linby, with the mill wheel still in position, 1928. In 1946 it was proposed to demolish the mill, and the draining of Papplewick Dam commenced. The mill was saved, however, and has been converted into two homes.

High Street, Hucknall, 1928. On the immediate left is James Hyde's drapery shop followed by a butcher, a corn dealer, a milliner and the Byron's Rest public house. On the right is William Challand's beer off-licence, and the shops beyond include two butchers, a tripe dealer, a grocer and the Hucknall Torkard Co-operative store. All these buildings have now been replaced by new premises.

Annesley Hall and church, 1933. The hall was the principal seat of the Chaworths and Chaworth-Musters, and knew both the young, love-sick Byron and the patronising Mary Chaworth. The house was deserted by the family in 1973 for the nearby Felley Priory, and subsequent owners have allowed it to fall into disrepair. In 1997 vandals almost gutted the property, which had already lost all its wooden panelling. To the right of the house is the ruined church, which was abandoned when a new church was built in Annesley in 1874.

Newstead Abbey, 1930. Eight centuries ago this so-called abbey – strictly speaking it should be called a priory – was built by Henry II to house a community of Canons Regular of the Order of St Augustine. Tradition holds that the gesture was made by the king in expiation for the crime of the murder of Thomas Becket in Canterbury Cathedral. The canons occupied Newstead for almost four hundred years, until the Dissolution of the Monasteries. Adjacent to the ruins of the abbey is the Tudor mansion inseparably linked with the Byron family, and particularly with the poet Byron, the last of the family to occupy Newstead.

A snowy landscape at Newstead Abbey. The road from Nottingham to Mansfield was often blocked by snow in the depth of winter, and the inhabitants of Newstead Abbey and other houses in the forest needed to be self-sufficient.

A gipsy bow-topped caravan on the road near Arnold, 1950. The gipsy appears to be asleep, while one of his children holds the reins of his horses. Meanwhile, his queen, in the trap behind, has no shelter from the rain. Now a rare sight, encampments of traditional gipsy caravans are occasionally seen in the more rural parts of the country.

A gipsy brings his bride home to his caravan in Daybrook, 1930. The groom is dressed in a suit with a velvet collar and the bride is wearing a dress trimmed with lace.

A party of schoolchildren splashing in the Day Brook, 1929. For the children this was a great treat, but for the teachers it was probably quite a headache.

Farrand's Mill, Daybrook, 1924. The mill was then already in decline and is now only a memory. The brook is mostly culverted today, ending the problems caused by the flooding of nearby land.

Blidworth Mill, 1935. The mill, which was built around 1816, was three storeys high and had four sails. The twentieth century saw a slow decline in its condition. During the First World War the mill was gutted for its scrap metal and by 1933 it had lost its sails. All that now remains is the ruined base.

Taking a break in a Blidworth farmyard: two hands find time for a chat. The fowls are contented, and the kitten peeping through the doorway is not sure whether to explore the farmyard.

A wintry scene on the River Maun near Clipstone.

Ollerton from the bridge over the River Maun, 1933 – a view which has not changed greatly. The building with the posters advertising films at the Picture House in New Ollerton is the public weighbridge. The film *There goes the Bride* starred Jessie Matthews, and *Wedding Rehearsal* starred Roland Young and George Grossmith. The building on the right was built in about 1680, and in the nineteenth century became the Blue Bell Inn.

A view towards St Giles' Church, Ollerton, 1933. Dowse's hardware shop is selling spades at *2s* and *3s 6d*, and the latest line in dolly tubs. Apart from Dowse's shop all these buildings remain, but the road now has speed humps to calm the traffic.

The Hop Pole Hotel, Ollerton, 1924. This is an eighteenth-century coaching inn, and a reminder of the hop-growing that survived in the area until the nineteenth century. The inn served the coach passengers travelling north who took the more picturesque route from Newark to Doncaster.

Manor Farm, on the right, is one of the oldest properties in Edwinstowe. It is believed it was built for the lord of the manor's agent. The upper storey and Tudor-style frontage were added about 150 years ago. The cottages on the left are Victorian, built in an earlier style. St Mary's Church in the background is by tradition supposed to be the scene of Robin Hood and Maid Marian's wedding.

Ranby Almshouses, 1926. Known in the past as the Malt Kiln and now as the Barracks, the house was occupied by old retainers of the Duke of Newcastle. The village of Ranby, with old houses by the Chesterfield Canal, has now been bypassed by the new A1 dual carriageway road.

Welbeck Abbey, 1930. The abbey is one of the ducal mansions built in Sherwood Forest during the two hundred years after the Dissolution of the Monasteries. The abbey was founded in 1153 by Thomas de Cuckney for the Premonstratensian Canons (White Canons). The present house is the product of nearly three centuries of building, culminating in the remodelling of the exterior of the house after a fire in 1902. Welbeck is famous for its subterranean rooms built by the 5th Duke of Portland, a shy recluse, who expended vast sums of money in rebuilding the house and laying out the grounds.

The gatehouse to Worksop Priory, 1933. The priory was founded by William de Lovetot in 1103 for a community of Augustinian or Black Canons. For centuries traffic passed through the archway of the gatehouse, until 1893–4 when, following the demolition of the adjoining blacksmith's forge, the road was diverted to the west side of the gatehouse, the upper room of which was used as a National School for many years but now houses an art gallery.

The Old Ship, Worksop, 1928. This timber-framed building is the oldest public house in Worksop and in the nineteenth century offered 'every convenience such as superior wines and liquors, well-aired beds and excellent stabling'. In 1850 the building was virtually halved in size, and the shop on the left built on the vacant land. That building has now been demolished and an extension in the original style has now been made to the Old Ship.

Children admiring the daffodils in a wood at Shireoaks. The village acquired its name from an ancient oak tree that once cast its shade into the three counties of Yorkshire, Derbyshire and Nottinghamshire.

Two young women taking a stroll down a lane near Hardwick on a bright spring day.

# North and West
# of the Trent

The view from Woodborough Hill, 1950. The landscape here of farmhouses and a patchwork of fields is as attractive as any in Nottinghamshire. In the foreground is Bank Farm, which after becoming a ruin has now been restored, and to the right is Fox Wood where a Roman settlement was discovered.

Two pretty girls picking tulips and daffodils at Thomas Robinson's nursery on Westdale Lane, Carlton, 1950.

A midday rest in a field at Gedling, 1932. On the left is Emmanuel Foster who was the organist at Woodborough church.

The church of All Hallows, Gedling, 1925. This part of the village, dominated by the church and now surrounded by suburbia, still retains some of its old character. Two of Nottinghamshire and England's greatest cricketers, Alfred Shaw and Arthur Shrewsbury, are buried in the churchyard here – though neither were natives of the village.

Holy Trinity Church, Lambley, 1926. The church was built in about 1460 by the will of Ralph Cromwell, Lord High Treasurer of England, who was born in Lambley in 1394. Lambley and cowslips, in the memories of local people, were inseparable, but sadly the flowers no longer bloom as prolifically as they once did.

Robert Harrison outside his cottage at Calverton, 1928. These cottages were built in 1834 by Windles Smith, and unlike most other stockingers' cottages they have their large windows on the ground floor. One row of the cottages was demolished in the 1960s, but the remainder were restored between 1972 and 1974. Robert Harrison knitted stockings for Princess Elizabeth, Princess Margaret and Princess Marina, and was still working when he was ninety years of age, three years before he died in 1938.

The Admiral Rodney, Calverton, 1925. The inn was named after Admiral George Brydes Rodney who was the victor over the French in the Battle of the Saints in 1782, which saved the West Indies for Britain. Common to many old inns, there is a tale of an underground passage, this one to the nearby Calverton Hall, and also stories of three ghosts – one a woman named Sarah who haunts the cellars.

The Manor House at Halloughton, 1930 – a house of three distinct parts and one of the oldest domestic buildings in the county that is still inhabited. The building on the right is a fourteenth-century peel tower built as a prebendary for Southwell Minster. Next to the tower house is a small Tudor farmhouse and on the left is an attractive Georgian farmhouse.

Thurgarton Priory, 1947. The church, which is all that remains of the Augustinian Priory, once possessed two towers and almost rivalled Southwell Minster for architectural grandeur. The priory was founded by Ralph d'Eyncourt between 1119 and 1139 for the safety of his soul. After Henry VIII closed the priory in 1538 it passed into the ownership of the Cooper family, but the monastic buildings were allowed to fall into disrepair. In 1777 John Gilbert Cooper built the present house, the ownership of which passed to two or three other families before becoming the Bishop of Southwell's palace from 1884 to 1909. Boots the Chemists purchased the priory in 1945, and used it as a veterinary research unit. When Boots sold the property in 1998 the hall was converted into apartments. One of the conditions of the sale was that the cricket pitch be let to the local club for fifty years, at a peppercorn rent of a bottle of linseed oil per year.

A wedding group outside the Coach and Horses, Thurgarton, 1912. The groom is Ernest Bentley and the bride Ida Fletcher, whose parents Henry and Emily Fletcher owned the public house. The groom's parents, Robert and Alice Bentley (on the left), lived at Manor Farm, Thurgarton. The bride is wearing a dress trimmed with Nottingham lace and the other ladies are all wearing splendid hats.

Ernest and Ida Bentley leaving the Coach and Horses, Thurgarton, in a Rolls-Royce for their honeymoon in London.

The crossroads in Thurgarton, *c.* 1955. John Fletcher is driving a Ferguson tractor from his father's farm in Bleasby Road on a fine summer's day. The smithy on the right, owned by John Milner, has now been pulled down and replaced by a sub-post office. The cottages in the background have since been incorporated into the Coach and Horses public house – just visible over the smithy.

The Red Lion, Thurgarton, 1948. This sixteenth-century inn was, in 1936, the scene of a brutal murder. The licensee of the inn, Sarah Clarke, was found in her bedroom with her throat cut and her niece Rebecca Clarke was discovered standing in a water trough outside the inn with a throat wound. Also in the trough was the dead woman's cat with a pound weight tied to its neck. The niece was later found guilty of murder but insane, and was committed to the City Mental Hospital.

The great west front of Southwell Minster. The first church on this site was established by the tenth century, but the present church was built in three stages between 1110 and 1290. The caps to the towers were rebuilt in 1880 to the original pattern, which they possessed until the fire of 1711. The minster is unsurpassed for the beauty of its stone carving, particularly in the chapter house. This is full of sculptured leaves of every variety of tree in Sherwood Forest.

Two boys admiring the massive stone pillars in the nave of Southwell Minster. The stonework, although dwarfing the boys, is so well-proportioned that the effect is not overpowering.

Children playing in a meadow near Southwell Minster, 1934. On the left is the Bishop's Palace and also the remains of the earlier palace, the outer walls of which survive as a walled garden. Southwell once had four famous wells, water from which was reputed to possess miraculous healing powers.

The Saracen's Head, Southwell, 1932. Once known as the King's Arms, the inn was established in the twelfth century and has been visited by ten monarchs, including most notably Charles I, who spent his last day of freedom here on 5 May 1646. A few days prior to the king's execution, Oliver Cromwell stayed at the Saracen's Head, and by an irony of fate slept in the same room that Charles had occupied.

The Ladies' Race at the Oxton Point-to-Point Meeting, 1937. The two riders on the right have jumped the fence successfully but the horse and rider on the left are taking a tumble.

The centre of Farnsfield, 1929. This view is virtually unchanged today, although the white house in the centre is no longer a farmhouse. On the left is the car park of the Red Lion, occupied by only one vehicle, and in the background is the nineteenth-century church of St Michael.

The grounds of Kirklington Hall, open to the public in 1930 under the Notts. Garden Scheme in aid of the Queen's Institute of District Nursing. The house is an eighteenth-century remodelling of an earlier property, although in 1904 further alterations were made.

The front of Kirklington Hall, 1930. The hall now houses the Rodney School, which was founded by Joan Thomas in 1944 in rooms at the Admiral Rodney in Southwell. The school moved to three other locations before becoming established here in 1954. Since then the school has acquired an international reputation, and pays particular attention to drama and dance – one former pupil was the choreographer Sir Kenneth MacMillan. In 1994 Joan Thomas handed over the role of principal to her daughter RoseAnna Howe, but is still using her skills in other spheres.

A small boy, seemingly in complete charge of a herd of sheep at Egmanton, 1924. The tiny thatched cottage has a brick extension, which has doubled its size.

Two men at the old craft of stacking hay at Egmanton – a ritual from the past.

151

Chewing a straw, a farmer leans contentedly on a gate at East Markham, 1952.

A team of horses pulling a tree-trunk at Askham, 1932. One tractor would now produce more power, but not the beauty of these five Forshaw shire horses.

Two ploughing teams in the flat landscape near Tuxford, 1928.

Tuxford Market Place, 1928. St Nicholas' Church dates from the fourteenth century but the town is largely Georgian. The house on the left, occupied by the grocers, J. Gale & Sons, was built in about 1795. The small building in the middle, a cobbler's shop owned by John Skelton, has now been demolished.

The Tuxford Twins, *c.* 1933. These windmills on Mill Mount, north of Tuxford, were both owned at one time by the Longbottom family. The post mill on the left was moved from Grassthorpe in 1874 and bought by Hugh Loughton-Longbottom in 1881. The mill continued in use until 1926 and was demolished in 1950. The tower mill was built in about 1820 and ceased production in 1927, having been severely damaged in a storm. David Ostick began restoring the mill in 1982 and by 1993 had returned it to full working order.

Ye Olde Sun Inn, Chapelgate, Retford, 1933. Once a house, it became an inn around 1750 and was one of several coaching inns serving the stage-coaches that ran on the Great North Road. Next door is Albert Flint's confectionery shop, which has now been pulled down.

Retford Town Hall, 1933. This ornate building was constructed in 1868, replacing an earlier hall. The building behind the war memorial is known as the Old Bank or Foljambe's, after Francis Foljambe who was a partner in Beckett's Bank there in the nineteenth century. In 1926 the Borough Council purchased the old bank premises and added the present frontage.

Blyth Hall and Church, 1930. The hall was built in the seventeenth century and occupied by the Mellish family for generations. During the Second World War it was taken over by the military and suffered serious damage. By the end of the war the hall had lost its roof, and it was demolished in 1972. The parish church has evidence of the nave and aisles of a Benedictine Priory, built by Roger de Builli in 1088. The numerous cars outside the hall indicate a meeting of the Grove Hunt.

Blyth Rectory with a bull-nose Morris car parked outside, 1930. The rectory was built by William Mellish in about 1770; the gardeners' cottages at each end are nineteenth-century additions.

The Rose and Crown Cottage at Blyth, 1930. This seventeenth-century house became an inn with a forge, stabling and a fodder room. When its licence was withdrawn the inn was purchased by George Glover, who was a motor engineer and later established a bus company running a service between Worksop and Langold. Customers at Glover's garage in those days had a choice of either Shell or Power petrol.

A Star automobile out for a sedate run in Blyth, 1908. Motor cars were still a novelty in the county, and the promenaders are amused and intrigued by the spectacle. Car owners were perhaps not always willing to take a back seat, but a chauffeur was almost obligatory.

# Acknowledgements and Picture Credits

I gratefully acknowledge the kindness of Mrs May Sentance and Miss Dorrie Stevenson – the daughters of Frank Stevenson – for generously allowing me to borrow their father's glass plates and prints, making this compilation of his photographs possible.

I would also like to thank Stella Middleton for permitting me to use her husband's photographs and also Geoff Blore, Hazel Mather, Jeff Sale and Elizabeth Staunton for kindly lending me prints from their personal collections.

I am indebted to Dorothy Ritchie and the staff of the Nottingham Local Studies Library for their help and kindness, and to the following who made the task of researching these photographs so pleasant and interesting:

David Bent, Elizabeth Brackenbury, Anthea Chalmers, Marylin Clarke, David and Jennifer Crane, Eddie and Jean Darke, Jen Eccles, Pat Greene, David and Vivien Little, Steve Lovatt, Jean Lowe, Julie Marsh, Alan Marshall, Georgina Ostick, William Peet, Mick Pickering, Peter and Catherine Player, Roy Plumb, Pamela Priestland, The Hon. Mrs George Seymour, Tony Shaw, David Slater, Martin and Jennifer Stinchcombe, Joan Thomas, Henry Tyler, David and Jennifer Walker, Tim Warner.

I also wish to thank my wife Margaret for all her help and support in the production of this book.

All photographs are by Frank Stevenson with the exception of the following (all numbers given are page numbers): Geoff Blore: 11, 13 top, 14 bottom, 15 top, 16 top, 17, 18 top, 21, 24 bottom, 42 top, 43 bottom, 88 bottom; The Boots Co. PLC: 49 bottom, 143 bottom; Co-operative Funeral Services: 15 bottom; Hazel Mather: 76 bottom; John (Jack) Middleton: 44, 45, 46, 47, 48, 50, 146; Nottingham Local Studies Library: 10, 35 bottom, 43 top, 69; Jeff Sale: 144, 145 top; Elizabeth Staunton: 63.

Nottingham-by-the-Sea, 1950. Skegness has been favoured by Nottinghamshire families for decades, and those loyal to the resort return year after year.

# Index

Frank Stevenson taking a well-earned rest.